Thomas Bewi
and Cherryburn

Northumberland

THE NATIONAL TRUST

His personal appearance was rustic; he was tall and powerfully formed, a quality which he was fond of displaying in his prime. His manners were somewhat rustic too, but he was shrewd, and disdained to ape the gentleman. His countenance was open and expressive, with a capacious forehead, strongly indicating intellect; his dark eyes beamed with the fire of genius.

J.J. AUDUBON, 1827

Above The Cat *from* A General History of Quadrupeds

Right Bewick in 1823; engraving after a portrait by James Ramsay

Ja.ˢ Ramsay Pinx.ᵗ

Henry Hoppner Meyer. Sculp.ᵗ

THE POET WHO LIVES ON THE BANKS OF THE TYNE

I…found him…playing with a group of curly rosy children, for whom he was drawing funny figures on a painted bench, and telling them the names of birds, insects, and plants… JOHN DOVASTON, 1827

…the Poet who lives on the banks of the Tyne,
Who has plied his rude tools with more fortunate toil
Than Reynolds e'er brought to his canvas and oil.
WORDSWORTH ON BEWICK

Britain has produced many much-loved book illustrators, but few have inspired such devotion as Thomas Bewick. And it all began at Cherryburn.

Bewick was born here in a humble cottage that still stands, and here he spent his childhood among the streams and fields of this beautiful landscape. Although he left for Newcastle at the age of fourteen, he never forgot Cherryburn, which inspired his fascination with nature and the ways of the world. These were the subject of the wood-engravings in his *A General History of Quadrupeds* and *A History of British Birds*, which made his name and fortune. His little vignettes recall the joys, terrors and mysteries of childhood.

The hands of a master

Engravers need steady hands. Bewick had a vice-like grip and the large, hardened hands of a blacksmith. Yet he was capable of the most extraordinarily delicate effects, bringing complete stories to life on a few square centimetres of boxwood. He could draw a portrait on his thumbnail, wipe it off with his tongue, and draw another just as quickly.

To authenticate his work, he would add a perfectly engraved facsimile of his own thumbprint.

Remembering Bewick

Cherryburn cherishes Thomas Bewick's memory at the place of his birth, protecting the landscape he loved, displaying the best of his work, and demonstrating how it was created.

Above Bewick stands on the banks of the Tyne, with Newcastle in the background. This portrait was engraved more than twenty years after Bewick's death, based on a painting by his friend James Ramsay

Left The Chillingham Bull, 1789, is the most famous of Bewick's single large wood engravings. It celebrates an old North Country strain of wild cattle in the more prestigious style of copper engraving. Although only 18.4 x 24.7cm, it required four boxwood blocks, which later opened up after being left in the sun, making perfect original impressions rare

3

I often, in a morning, set off stark naked *across the fell, where I was joined by some associates, who, in like manner, ran about like mad things.* BEWICK'S MEMOIR

The margins of my books, and every space of spare and blank paper, became filled with various kinds of devices or scenes I had met with. BEWICK

Above Bewick's vignettes recall his childhood at Cherryburn

Opposite top Cherryburn today. Bewick was born in the cottage in the centre

Opposite below Bewick's father, John, ran a nearby coal mine, one of many that brought prosperity to the region. His brother's engraving appeared in John Trusler's *The Progress of Man and Society*, 1791

Thomas Bewick was born at Cherryburn in August 1753 (the precise day is uncertain). The son of a farmer, who also leased a mine, he was the eldest of eight children.

Thomas was a strong-minded boy and a compulsive artist: 'I spent as much time as I could find in filling with my pencil all the unoccupied spaces [on his writing slate], with representations of such objects as struck my fancy.' When he was not doodling in his school books, he was playing truant, exploring the rolling countryside around Cherryburn. He was particularly drawn to water, making dams and sailing toy boats in the streams that run through the valley. In spring and summer he loved to fish for salmon, which still filled the Tyne. He believed that 'angling ought to be indulged in unchecked by arbitrary laws, as the birthright of every one (but particularly of the sedentary & studious) for ever.' And

children (girls included) should be allowed to *romp*.

Bewick's relatively humble origins and open-air childhood earned him the reputation of an untutored genius. But in fact he was well educated, thanks to the Revd Christopher Gregson of nearby Ovingham parsonage, from whom he acquired the deeply moral outlook that colours his vignettes.

Leaving Cherryburn

In 1767 Bewick was fourteen. His childhood was over, and it was time to leave Cherryburn. But he did so with regret: 'I can only say my heart was like to break; and, as we passed away, I inwardly bade farewell to the winny wilds, to Mickley bank, to the Stob-cross hill, to the water-banks, the woods, and to particular trees.'

THE PLACE OF MY NATIVITY
'Cherryburn House, the place of my nativity, and which for many years my eyes beheld with cherished delight, is situated on the south bank of the Tyne, in the county of Northumberland, a short distance from the river. The house, stables, etc., stand on the west side of a little dean [valley], at the foot of which runs a burn.' Cherryburn in 1838. Detail from an engraving by Bewick's pupil, John Jackson

Newcastle upon Tyne Races.

Top Even straightforward jobs like this trade card show Bewick's skill at depicting vegetation. In the background can be seen the distinctive spire of St Nicholas church, which overlooked the Beilby workshop

Above Bewick did much routine work, including the illustration for this handbill advertising a race meeting on the Town Moor. He enjoyed taking his family to the races, filling his pockets with nuts for the children

Bewick was apprenticed to Ralph Beilby, who ran the leading engraving workshop in Newcastle. Beilby's bread-and-butter work was engraving of every kind: 'Our work place was filled with the coarsest kinds of steel stamps – pipe Moulds – Bottle moulds – Brass Clock faces – Door plates – Coffin plates – Bookbinders Letters & stamps, Steel, Silver & gold Seals – Mourning Rings – Arms crests & cyphers on silver & every kind of job, from the Silver Smiths – writing engraving of Bills, bank notes, Bills of parcels, shop bills & cards.'

Newcastle: town of wealth and learning

The Beilby workshop was kept busy as the town prospered. Newcastle's population of 25,000 still lived within its medieval walls, but the coal from the Tyneside mines that passed through the town's wharves was transforming the place. Wealth stimulated local pride and intellectual life: late 18th-century Newcastle supported new assembly rooms, three newspapers, a thriving book trade and almost 50 societies and clubs, where high-minded men of business like Bewick could put the world to rights.

Learning his trade

Ralph Beilby proved an ideal teacher. Bewick thought him 'the best master in the World for learning Boys, for he obliged them to put their hands to every variety of work'. Bewick showed an immediate aptitude for engraving on wood, but this was always a relatively small part of the business. Most of his time was spent engraving lettering on copper and silver. It was Bewick himself who later engraved the emblem of the anti-slavery movement on to a silver tea-urn and salver now on show at Wallington (also owned by the National Trust).

Home and away

Cherryburn remained close to his heart. After a hard day's work in Newcastle, he thought nothing of walking the eleven miles back home, and when he completed his apprenticeship in 1774, he returned to live there. He spent the summer of 1776 walking 500 miles across Scotland, which he loved. That autumn, he travelled south to London, which he hated: 'It appeared to me to be a World of itself where every thing in the extreme, might at once be seen – extreme riches – extreme poverty – extreme Grandeur & extreme wretchedness.' He returned to the North East with relief the following year and remained there for the rest of his life. In 1777 Bewick went into partnership with his old master – a partnership that was to last two decades.

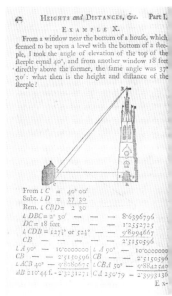

Above The technical illustrations in Charles Hutton's *Treatise on Mensuration*, 1768, were one of Bewick's first apprentice jobs. St Nicholas church again features

Left Engraving coffin plates taught Bewick the demanding art of cutting lettering in metal (Tyne & Wear Museums)

Opposite Thomas Bewick at the age of about 27, painted by his Newcastle friend George Gray

HOW DID HE DO IT?

BEWICK'S TECHNIQUE

His delicate and beautiful tools were all made by himself, and I may with truth say that his shop was the only artist's 'shop' that I ever found perfectly clean and tidy. J.J. AUDUBON, 1827

Above Bewick's original boxwood block for the Hyena and a proof taken from it; from *A General History of Quadrupeds*, 1790. The relief 'peaks' (grey on the block) print black

Below The Titlark. One of Bewick's beautiful preparatory watercolours

Preparation

For the book illustrations that made his name, Bewick began by preparing delicate pencil drawings (often embellished with colour), which are works of art in their own right. He rubbed the back of the sheet all over with a soft lead pencil, then placed it face-up on the engraving block, and traced over the outline of the design to transfer it to the block. Only then could he begin cutting.

Cutting

Bewick's engraving method was determined by the fact that his illustrations were to be printed with type. On each piece of type, the letter form stood in relief and when inked up, printed black. Bewick made his wood engravings in a similar way. Traditionally, engravings of this kind were cut with simple tools, using planks of soft wood that had been sliced *along the grain*. They could be large, but were often crude. Bewick, however, chose to engrave on blocks of boxwood that had been cut *across the grain*. So they were small (no more than about 12cm in diameter), but because this close-grained timber was immensely hard-wearing, Bewick could use the finer tools he employed for engraving metal: 'some broad gouges for wide excavations; some narrow, for fine wide lines;

and some many pointed for parallels, which either straight or wavy, he cut with great rapidity'. He rested the block on a convex leather pad so that it could be easily turned when cutting curved lines. In this way he achieved the delicate and precise effects of the copper engraver.

This is all the more remarkable in that engraving on metal is an entirely different process, known as *intaglio*, in which it is the engraved lines that print black, not the main surface (from which the ink has to be wiped away with coarse muslin before every impression). As a result, copper engravings can rapidly lose their crispness. By contrast, Bewick's boxwood blocks could withstand huge numbers of printings. He calculated that his little view of Newcastle for a newspaper had taken over 900,000 impressions.

Even more remarkably, the immensely taxing work for his own books was done at the end of a long day, often by candlelight.

Printing

Cutting the blocks was only half the battle; it was just as vital that they were printed properly. This was a struggle, as Bewick himself admitted: 'The first difficulty, I felt, as I proceeded, was in getting the cuts I had done, printed so as to look any thing like my

drawings, on the blocks of wood, nor in
corresponding to the labour, I had bestowed
upon the cutting of the designs.' The Beilby
workshop had two presses for printing copper
engravings, but nothing suitable for book
work. Anxious to keep control of his blocks,
Bewick entrusted the work to local
Newcastle printers, but they were more used
to speedy printing of handbills than fine book
illustrations. Reproducing the subtlety of his
engravings required the right kind of paper
properly dampened, and the right kind of
stiff ink applied in just the right quantity.
To ensure that his atmospheric landscape
backgrounds printed the correct shade of
grey, Bewick carefully lowered the relief in
these parts of the block so that the paper took
up less ink in the impression.

The beasts and birds which enlivened the beautiful scenery of woods and wilds surrounding my native hamlet, furnished me with an endless supply of subjects. BEWICK

I…date the Quadrupeds to be the commencement of Wood Engraving worthy of attention. Before that I was engaged in the general work of a Country Engraver Shop; one hour employed on Copper, another on Wood, another on Silver, another on Brass, another on Steel – indeed ready and willing to undertake any description of work. BEWICK

Above **The Red Deer**

Right top **The Walrus**

Right **The Elephant**

A GENERAL HISTORY OF QUADRUPEDS

Having from the time that I was a school Boy, been displeased with most of the cuts in children's books, & particularly with those of the 'Three Hundred Animals' the figures of which, even at that time, I thought I could depicture much better than those in that Book; and having afterwards, very often turned the matter over in my mind, of making improvements in that publication – I at last came to the determination of commencing the attempt. BEWICK

Bewick's childhood explorations of the countryside around Cherryburn had left him with a love of the local fauna. This was also the age of the Enlightenment ('the march of intellect', as Bewick called it), when people were beginning to classify the natural world and to look at animals with more understanding and sympathy.

Bewick first mentioned his idea for a new illustrated survey of four-footed animals in 1781, the year that Thomas Pennant published his own *General History of Quadrupeds*. Ever a careful man, Bewick hesitated, as the Beilby workshop was not set up to print or publish books. However, he was encouraged by his friend, Solomon Hodgson, a successful bookseller and printer and the editor of the *Newcastle Chronicle*, who was impressed by Bewick's engravings. Hodgson convinced Bewick that a market existed for such a work – indeed several markets: the children's book he had originally envisaged, in a standard format; and a grander edition for collectors. To spread the risk, Bewick offered copies for sale not only in Newcastle, but also through a London wholesaler and by advance subscription.

Bewick began work in earnest in November 1785 – on the day his father died. 'I made sketches, first from memory, & then corrected & finished the drawings upon the Wood, from a second examination of the different subjects.' In all, he represented 199 animals. Although the poses are generally static and similar, Bewick had an uncanny ability to capture character, and the landscape backgrounds are packed with detail and varied to suggest the appropriate habitat. After five years' labour, the *Quadrupeds* was published in April 1790 and was an immediate success. The first printing of 1,600 copies sold out in months, and the book went through eight editions in his lifetime.

Above Bewick's workshop in St Nicholas churchyard

Below An opening from the printed book, with one of Bewick's original boxwood blocks for it

VIGNETTES

I interspersed the more serious studies with Tale-*pieces of gaiety and humour; yet even in these seldom without an endeavour to illustrate some truth, or point some moral.* BEWICK

Above Cat and mouse vignette

Below right It was a small vignette, cut on a block of boxwood not more than two by three inches in surface, and represented a dog frightened at night by what he fancied to be living objects, but which were actually roots and branches of trees, rocks and other objects bearing the semblance of men. This curious piece of art, like all his works, was exquisite.

J.J. AUDUBON, 1827

Far right A suicide. One of the more morbid vignettes to which Charlotte Brontë's Jane Eyre was drawn

Opposite An opening from *Quadrupeds*, showing how the vignettes were used to fill up the space left at the end of the text descriptions

The little tail-pieces or vignettes in Bewick's *Quadrupeds* originally had a mundane practical purpose – to fill the space left at the end of the extended captions that accompany his animal illustrations. But from the start they were what attracted readers.

The passages describing Bewick's country childhood at Cherryburn are the liveliest part of his *Memoir*, and it was this that inspired his vignettes. Many depict the simple pleasures of childhood in a Northumbrian landscape still unscarred by the Industrial Revolution. The mood is nostalgic, but direct, and often has a darker, didactic edge. Bewick wanted his young readers to absorb the 'Great Truths of Creation': life is short and full of peril; human pride and folly bring disaster; and nature is a reflection of the divine purpose. The tale is often told through allegory, drawing on a traditional fable of the kind that Bewick had known since childhood.

Unlike the animal illustrations, Bewick's vignettes are not captioned, but their message is all the more powerful for not being spelt out.

An attentive reader

On a drear November day the young Jane Eyre is sitting by a window, unhappy and alone. In her lap lies a copy of Bewick's *History of British Birds*. Like most of his readers, she is less interested in the text than in the little vignettes, and particularly the more morbid ones which seem to chime with her mood: 'Each picture told a story; mysterious to my undeveloped understanding and imperfect feelings, yet ever profoundly interesting.'

will die rather than defert them. Wounds ferve only to make the attachment more violent. They embrace their cubs to the laft, and bemoan them with the moft piteous cries.

These creatures feed on fifh, feals, and the carcafes of whales; are fond of human blood; and are fo fearlefs, as to attack companies of armed men, and even to board fmall veffels. Allured by the fcent of feals flefh, they often break into the huts of the Greenlanders. They fometimes attack the Morfe; with which they have terrible conflicts: But the large teeth of that animal give it a decided fuperiority over the Bear, which is generally worfted.

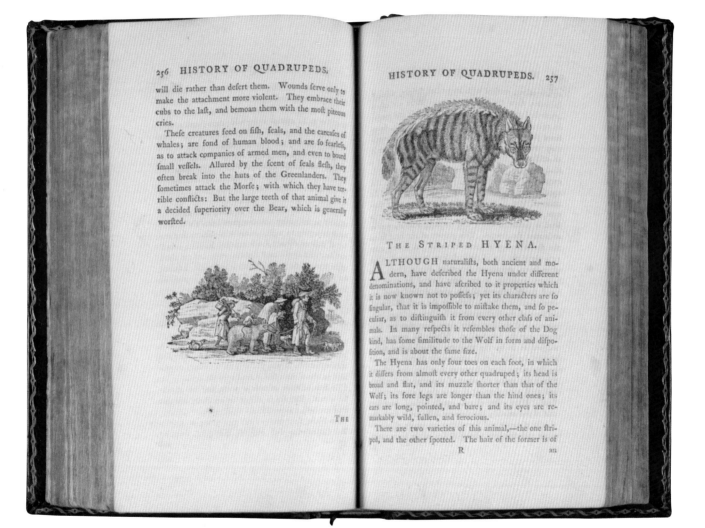

THE

The Striped HYENA.

ALTHOUGH naturalifts, both ancient and modern, have defcribed the Hyena under different denominations, and have afcribed to it properties which it is now known not to poffefs; yet its characters are fo fingular, that it is impoffible to miftake them, and fo peculiar, as to diftinguifh it from every other clafs of animals. In many refpects it refembles thofe of the Dog kind, has fome fimilitude to the Wolf in form and difpofition, and is about the fame fize.

The Hyena has only four toes on each foot, in which it differs from almoft every other quadruped; its head is broad and flat, and its muzzle fhorter than that of the Wolf; its fore legs are longer than the hind ones; its ears are long, pointed, and bare; and its eyes are remarkably wild, fullen, and ferocious.

There are two varieties of this animal,—the one ftriped, and the other fpotted. The hair of the former is of

R   an

colour. The quill feathers are black, the inner webs
crossed or spotted with white: the tail is barred with
black, on a white ground ringed with red: the thighs
are bare about half way above the knee ......uish colour, and the toes are thick.................er side,
being furnished with............................side
to the ....

....t parts of
Euro..........................anean Islands. In
Britai................ce is upon the large, heathy,
boggy ....re they breed. Their food consists of
worms, ...s, and insects, which they pick out of the soft
mossy ground by the marshy pools, which are common
in such places. In winter they depart to the sea-side,
where they are seen in great numbers, and then live upon the worms, marine insects, and other fishy substances
which they pick up on the beach, and among the loose
rocks and pools left by the retiring tide. The flesh of
the Curlew has been characterised by some as very good,
and of a fine flavour; by others as directly the reverse:

the truth is, that while they are in health and season, and
live on the moors, scarcely any bird can excel them in
goodness; but when they have lived some time on the
sea-shore, they acquire a rank and fishy taste.

THE WHIMBREL.

(*Scolopax Phæopus*, Lin.—*Le petit Courlis*, Buff.)

THE Whimbrel is only about half the size of the Curlew, which it very nearly resembles in shape, the colours
of its plumage, and manner of living. It is about seven-
teen inches in length, and twenty-nine in breadth, and
weighs about fourteen ounces. The bill is about three
inches long, the upper mandible black, the under one
pale red. The upper part of the head is black, divided
in the middle of the crown by a white line from the
brow to the hinder part: between the bill and the eyes
there is a darkish oblong spot: the sides of the head, the

An opening from *Land Birds*

14

Birds, their nests, their eggs, and their young…to me were long a source of great delight, and many a spring morning I watched and looked after them. BEWICK

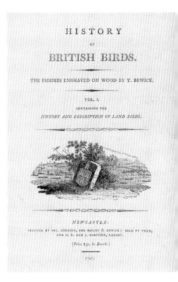

Land Birds

Bewick conceived the idea for an illustrated history of birds in 1786, but with typical caution did not start work until he had seen the success of *Quadrupeds*. It began as a guide to all the world's birds, but he soon realised that this was too ambitious. So he restricted the first volume to British land birds. He certainly looked at the illustrations in similar guides by Pennant, Latham and others, but preferred to work directly from nature. He spent two months in 1791 drawing from the stuffed specimens in the private museum of the late Marmaduke Tunstall (now in the Hancock Museum in Newcastle). However, he was unhappy with the results:

> I had not been long thus engaged 'till I found the very great difference between preserved Specimens & those from nature, no regard having been paid at that time to place the former in their proper attitudes, nor to place the different series of the feathers, so as to fall properly upon each other. This has always given me a great deal of trouble to get at the markings of the dishevelled plumage & when done with every pains, I never felt satisfied with them. I was on this account driven to wait for Birds newly shot, or brought to me alive, and in the intervals employed my time in designing & engraving tailpieces or Vignettes.

Land Birds was published in 1797. A more scholarly work than *Quadrupeds*, it achieved even greater success, but provoked a row with his business partner. Ralph Beilby insisted on receiving sole credit as the author of the book, although Bewick had extensively revised the text. With equal stubbornness, Bewick refused to give Beilby any credit. The twenty-year partnership split up, with Beilby retaining the enamelling and watchglass side of the business, while Bewick took on the engraving enterprises.

Water Birds

'As soon as each Bird was finished in the Wood, I set about describing it from my Specimen – and at the same time consulted every Authority I could meet with to know what had been said, & this together with what I knew from my own knowledge, were then compared, and in this way I finished, as truly as I could, the second volume of the History of British Birds.'

Bewick worked on alone on the second volume of *British Birds*, which was devoted to aquatic species and was finally published in July 1804.

Top The title-page for the first edition of the first volume of the *History of British Birds*. Arguments between Bewick and Beilby over the credit for the authorship of this volume brought an end to their partnership

Above The Black-headed Gull; from *Water Birds*

FABLES

*I could not help regretting that I had not published a Book, similar to 'Croxall's Esops Fables'…
I thought with better executed designs, it would impart the same delight to others, that I had
experienced from attentively reading it.* BEWICK

*Above The Drunken
Husband*, from *The Fables
of Aesop*, 1818

Right In 1818 Bewick issued
a receipt with every copy
sold of *The Fables of Aesop*.
As a security measure and
show of virtuosity, he
engraved a perfect replica
of his own thumbprint on
it. For good measure, he
then overprinted the
seaweed on his in-house
copper engraving press

The traditional fables of Aesop had been part
of Bewick's life since his earliest days. So it
was natural that he should want to publish his
own edition. He conceived the book during
one of his rare illnesses in 1812, and, now in
his sixties, the close work was starting to cause
him eye problems:

> The execution of the fine work of the Cuts,
> during the day light, was very trying to the
> Eyes, & the compiling or writing the Book by
> candle light in my Evenings at home, together
> injured the Optic nerve & that put the rest of
> the nerves out of tune, so that I was obliged,
> for a short time to leave off this application.

He was obliged to rely on his pupils to cut
the blocks, although he himself continued to
conceive the designs and supervise every stage
of the work. He also had problems with the
printing, when the wrong kind of paper was
used: 'I am sorry to find that too many of the
Impressions of the Cuts of Esops Fables are
ragged and grey and have none of the softness
& smoothness which Wood Cuts will exhibit,
when properly printed.'

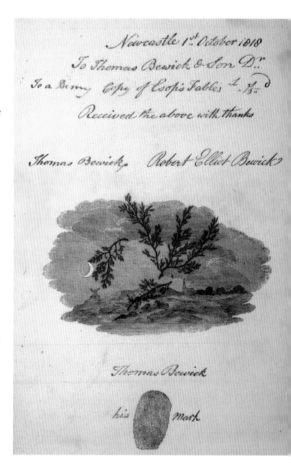

The Fox and Grapes; from
The Fables of Aesop, 1820

Right North View of St Nicholas Church, Newcastle; watercolour by Robert Johnson, about 1790–6 (Tyne & Wear Museums)

Opposite top The seated figure on the right is playing the Northumbrian pipes in this business card engraved by Bewick for a Newcastle dancing master

Opposite below A vignette by Luke Clennell, who was perhaps Bewick's most talented pupil

APPRENTICES

Bewick had had a traditional apprenticeship, and when he became his own master, he debated whether to work alone. But running a busy engraving workshop required a large team, and so he was obliged to take on apprentices, usually in their late teens for a period of seven years.

In his *Memoir*, Bewick devoted considerable space to the most dedicated of his pupils. He was closest to his easy-going younger brother, **John Bewick** (1760–95), who went on to carve out a very successful career in London as an illustrator of children's books. John's delicate health was wrecked by his carousing, and he died comparatively young of tuberculosis. Thomas took great pride in John's achievements and was always careful to acknowledge his brother's part in establishing the Bewick name.

Robert Johnson (1770–96) was a highly talented draughtsman and 'super-excellent' watercolourist, who did much of the preparatory work for *British Birds*. Like John Bewick, he suffered from poor health, which Thomas Bewick attempted to cure with a spartan diet of rye bread and water, unsuccessfully.

John Jackson (1801–48) came from the nearby village of Ovingham and showed great skill in interpreting the designs of others through his engravings. He conceived and cut the illustrations for W.A. Chatto's *Treatise on Wood Engraving* (1839), which did much to spread understanding of Bewick's technique.

BEWICK AND MUSIC

Bewick would whistle while he worked at his bench, a habit he had probably picked up from his father, whose loud whistle used to call him home as a child. He was proud to be described as 'the best whistler in England', but not everyone was so complimentary. His aunt, Mrs Blackett, with whom he lodged while an apprentice in Newcastle, banned him from whistling or making any other kind of music in her house. Despite this, he campaigned for whistling competitions at local fairs: 'contests of this agreeable kind would be found to throng the place and give a new character of cheerfulness to these meetings'. Cherryburn keeps alive his enthusiasm by holding an annual whistling competition.

Bewick had a natural ear for a tune and particularly loved the traditional songs and melodies of the Borders, as played on the Northumbrian pipes, which he did much to promote.

MR KINLOCH'S BALL

I used to contrive... to engage John Peacock, our inimitable performer to play on the Northumberland or small pipes, and with his old tunes, his lilts, his pauses & his variations, I was always excessively pleased. At one time I was afraid, that these old Tunes and this Ancient Instrument, might from neglect of encouragement get out of use, and I did every thing in my power to prevent this. BEWICK

LAST YEARS

[Bewick] was a tall stout man, with a large head, and with his eyes placed farther apart than those of any man I had ever seen: – a perfect old Englishman, full of life, although seventy-four years of age, active and prompt in his labours. J.J. AUDUBON, 1827

Right Bewick's memorial in nearby Ovingham church

Below Ovingham church. Bewick designed the gravestone for his beloved brother John in the churchyard, 'where I hope, when my *Glass* is run out to be laid down beside him'

Opposite Waiting for Death. A starving horse stands by a lightning-struck tree. This is one of Bewick's grimmest and (at 22.2 x 29.2 cm) largest engravings. It was left unfinished at his death and finally printed up by Robert Bewick only in 1832

History of British Fishes

A book on fish was a natural successor to *Quadrupeds* and *British Birds*, particularly for an expert fisherman like Bewick. The publication was announced in 1826, sixteen species and numerous vignettes were engraved, and delicate preparatory drawings for many more were produced by Thomas's son, Robert. But by then Bewick was too frail to complete the book, and his son too wanting in confidence. He also spoke of the difficulty that came from catching the likenesses of fish, as they lost their freshness and iridescence so swiftly.

The *Memoir*

Bewick's last years were taken up with overseeing revised editions of the *Quadrupeds* and *British Birds* and with writing his autobiography. Bewick was by then a celebrity, and the *Memoir*, which was addressed to his daughter Jane, was designed to set down his own account of his life. It was not, however, published until 1862, many years after his death on 8 November 1828. Bewick was buried in Ovingham churchyard less than a mile across the valley from his birthplace.

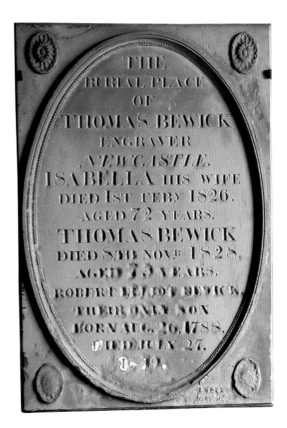

RE Bewi

ROBERT BEWICK (1788–1849)

Bewick's only son, Robert, lived always in the shadow of his famous and strong-willed father. It did not help that he was cripplingly shy and often in poor health. Despite this, Robert Bewick was an exceptional draftsman and watercolourist who produced numerous delicate preparatory designs for the abortive *History of British Fishes*. As Thomas Bewick explained, 'I am now not so well able, as I used to be, to run about seeking Specimens, and am obliged to trust to the exertions of my son who, from the accuracy & beauty of his drawings cannot be surpassed.' Many of these drawings now belong to the Natural History Society of Northumbria and the British Museum.

Robert Bewick was also a skilled performer on the Northumbrian pipes, when he could be prevailed on to play in public. The painter William Bell Scott remembered him as 'a heavy slouching, able-bodied countryman, as I thought, about fifty-five or so, with an absent, bewildered expression of face, the snow still lying white on his penthouse eyebrows':

> Robert was one of the last remaining adepts on the small Northumbrian bagpipes, and we were shortly after invited to take tea at a friend's house for the purpose of hearing him. He appeared carrying the union pipes under his arm, accompanied by two tall old-fashioned maiden sisters; but when the time arrived for his performance, he seemed as scared as some men are who have to make a public speech, and was evidently inclined to run away. Our host, however, who knew him well, proposed that he should tune his instrument on the landing outside the drawing-room door, which was a formula he appeared to understand; and after the tuning he played there, and we heard him perfectly, and applauded him much. The ice thus broken, he soon gained confidence, re-entered the room, and walked about excitedly playing Scottish airs with variations in the loveliest manner on that most delicate of native instruments.

Above Robert Bewick's engraving tools, which he may have inherited from his father

Left Bewick's sketch of his son Robert playing the Northumbrian pipes in the margin of his cash book

Opposite A preparatory pencil study of a John Dory by Robert Bewick for *British Fishes* (British Museum)

RESCUING CHERRYBURN

In June 1828 Bewick wrote to a friend: 'I have lately been spending a few days in visiting the place of my nativity & the scenes of many happy days (but the House in which I was born is I fear agoing to be pulled down – it is very old)'.

Above The cottage kitchen drawn by Robert Bewick in 1844

Right The workshop at Cherryburn demonstrates how Bewick engraved and printed his work

Below Cherryburn now possesses a superb collection of Bewick's publications acquired with the generous help of the National Heritage Memorial Fund from the New York book dealer and collector Justin Schiller. It also preserves 150 of the original blocks and important manuscripts

One end of the cottage was pulled down, but the rest survived, perhaps because in the late 1820s the family of Thomas Bewick's youngest brother William decided to build a larger, more comfortable house across the farmyard. In the 1840s Robert Bewick recorded the interior of the old cottage in meticulous drawings which have guided the modern reconstruction. The house comprised a kitchen, small and large sitting rooms, a

dairy and a bedroom upstairs. At the heart of the house was the kitchen range, which not only cooked food, but also heated the building and water for the tin hip-bath in which the young Bewick would have washed.

The Bewick Birthplace Trust

In 1982 the Cherryburn estate came on the market. The still unspoilt character of Bewick's birthplace encouraged a group of enthusiasts under the energetic leadership of Frank Atkinson and Iain Bain to set up a charitable trust to acquire Cherryburn. It had four aims:

- to acquire and present Bewick's works for the benefit of the public

- to re-create an experience of 18th-century rural life

- to preserve a historic landscape as an amenity for local people

- to provide facilities for study and research into the history of engraving and printing

The National Trust, which took on responsibility for Cherryburn in 1991, endeavours to fulfil these objectives.